THE STORY OF
YOUNG DAVID
YAH'S ANOINTED

by The Mysterious Prester John

Text Copyright © 2021 by Prester John

All rights reserved. No part of this book may be reproduced, scanned, or distributed in any printed or electronic form or by any means without prior written consent of the publisher, except for brief quotes used in reviews. Please do not participate in or encourage piracy of copyrighted materials in violation of the author's rights. Purchase only authorized editions.

Published by Hadassah's Crown Publishing, LLC

Library of Congress Catalog Number: 2021922428

ISBN 978-1-950894-60-4

Printed in the United States

This Book Belongs to

_____

In the ancient land of Israel, there ruled a strong king.
He was adored by the citizens of his nation. Oh his praises they did sing.
His name was King Saul, and he ruled his territory with a firm gripped hand. He defeated all of Israel's enemies, who dwelt in neighboring lands.

But as Saul's popularity grew, he became increasingly disobedient. He ignored Israel's God, Yah, and the prophets couldn't stand to see it. "King Saul, you must repent!" the prophet Samuel warned. "Ha...oh Samuel, don't be foolish," the haughty King Saul scorned."

For days, the prophet Samuel mourned over King Saul's foolish pride. For the king was Yah's anointed, once the apple of God's eye. Then Yah called out to Samuel, "How long will Saul cause you to grieve? Israel's next king resides in Bethlehem, and you'll ensure that my anointing he does receive."

The next day Samuel headed for Jesse's house, where he was instructed to go. He commanded the guards to "wait outside," for his true mission he did not want them to know.

Samuel knocked on the wooden door, and Jesse answered to a surprise; for at that moment he learned that within his home, did Israel's next king reside!

Jesse hurried and gathered seven of his sons to introduce to Israel's High Priest. Samuel was particularly impressed with Eliab, for he stood out as chief!

However, Yah rejected all the sons that Jesse had brought forth, for our God measures a man differently than we do here on Earth.

Samuel then approached Jesse to see if maybe he had another son. Jesse paused, thought, then proclaimed that indeed there was another one.

Jesse's young son David played music while tending his father's sheep. The royal guards couldn't help but enjoy his songs as they tapped their dancing feet.

The prophet Samuel approached young David, delivering the amazing news, that David was in fact Yah's chosen, and that one day he'd fill King Saul's shoes.

Samuel proceeded with the ceremony and in despair, King Saul grabbed his head. As Yah's anointing passed from him to David, Saul was left with a bad spirit instead.

David's family looked on in admiration, as the young man received Yah's anointing. But quietly they wondered in silence, when David would become the new king.

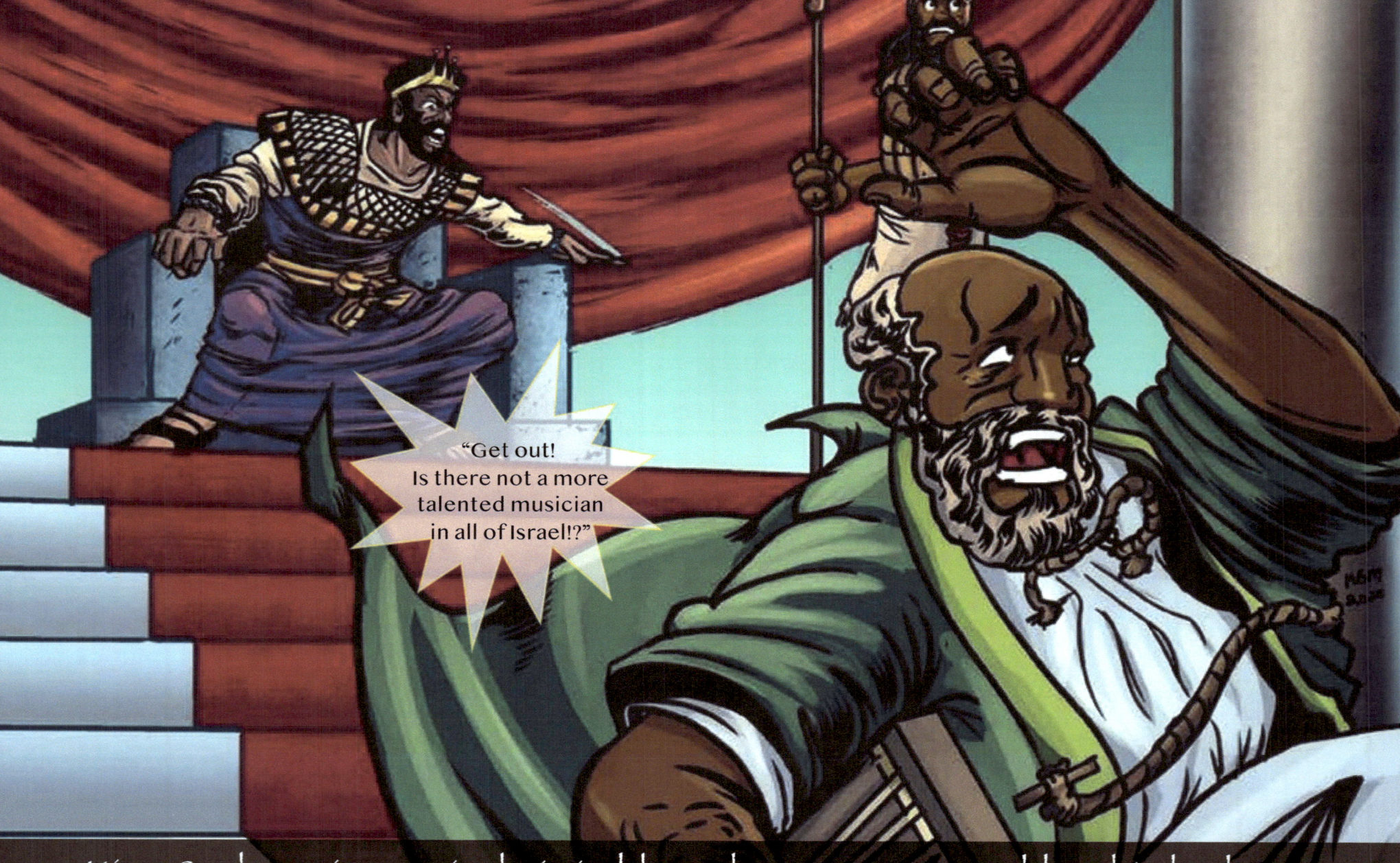

King Saul was increasingly irritable as he was tormented by this bad spirit. He sought music to soothe his tortured soul, but he erupted violently every time he'd hear it.

One of the royal guards remembered young David and approached the king with an idea. "There's a great musician that resides in Bethlehem, perhaps you'd like me to bring him here?"

David was summoned to the king's chambers, where he sang a soothing ballad. As he sang, one thing became increasingly clear...that this young man certainly had talent!

His music was a success as Saul's bad spirit became sedated. And as the king's daughter locked eyes with David, they both became infatuated.

Sometime later, peace was thwarted as hostile forces came from the North. It was a Philistine invasion, and from their ranks a monster did step forth.

"I am Goliath, the greatest of all warriors and a champion amongst all man. But if one of you is brave enough to fight me, and wins, we promise to leave your land."

He was the mighty Goliath, the giant of Philistia, who stood over 9 feet tall. He disrespected Israel's God, and threatened to enslave all who served King Saul.

King Saul assembled his army to defend against the Philistine invasion. David's brothers enlisted in the military in order to fight for their threatened nation.

David's sadness was replaced by a fiery resolve, as he determined what he'd do. David would face the giant himself and prove that the God of Israel was true!

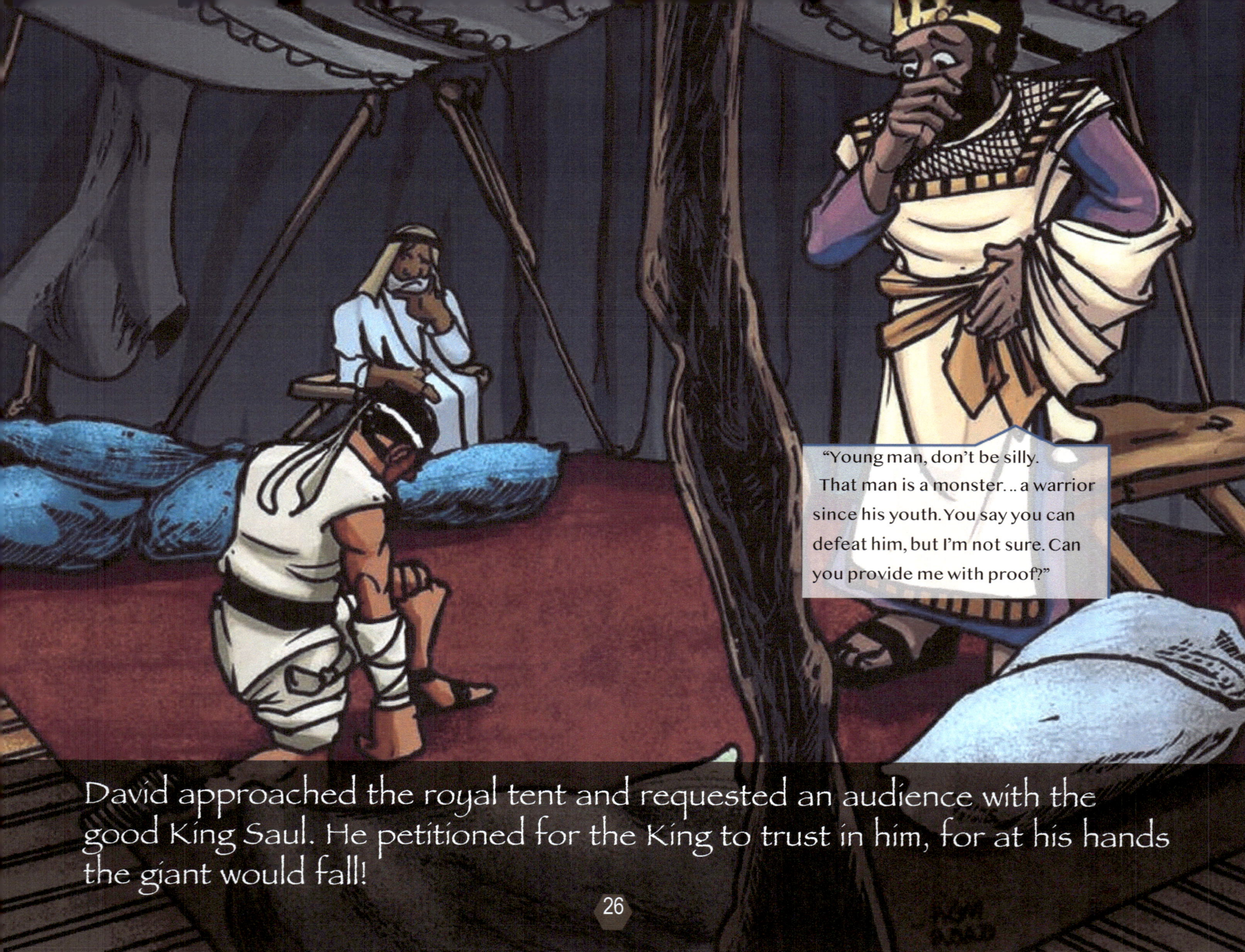

David approached the royal tent and requested an audience with the good King Saul. He petitioned for the King to trust in him, for at his hands the giant would fall!

David told stories about defending his flock from predators that dared advance. Lions, bears, it did not matter... none of them stood a chance!

As David approached the giant, he felt Yah's presence and knew that he was not alone. But Goliath chuckled and asked, "Am I a dog, that you come at me with sticks and stones?"

David landed a devastating blow and the giant was defeated! The Philistine army couldn't believe their eyes. They gasped and then quickly retreated.

He did it... he actually did it! David saved the nation! The people cheered and carried him back into town to celebrate this momentous occasion!

The people cheered and sang praises of David that were heard wide and far. But as the crowds celebrated, the king's bad spirit returned, as he became jealous of Israel's newfound star.

Acknowledgments

The team at Key of David Bible Stories would like to issue a special thank you to:

Pastor Omar Thibeaux &
Philadelphia Christian Church

Your dedication to spreading the Word of Our Father Yah and the gospel of His Son, Yahshua, has been an inspiration to many. Additionally, your support for this project means more than you know! May Yah continue to bless you and your ministry.

Meet the Team

Author: Preston Johnson

Bio: Preston is a husband and father who was inspired to create the Key of David Bible Stories series due to a desire to positively impact children with powerful stories and imagery from the Bible. Preston was born and raised in the town of Pottstown, PA, which is a blue-collar community located west of Philadelphia. As a young man, he was a member of
Bethel AME Church and developed a passion for art and community service, as he participated in two collaborative mural arts projects located at the Ricketts Community Center and the Pottstown Public Library.

Illustrator: Kenneth Brian Moore

Bio: Kenneth is an experienced illustrator and Graphic Designer who is currently based in Nashville, TN. Since graduating cum laude from Nossi College of Art in 2012, he has worked with an array of reputable businesses, ad agencies, collaborations with other creatives, and various entrepreneurs, placing a consistent focus on the impact of his client's goals on their audience. Inspired by Filmation, Ruby-Spears, Don Bluth, and Rankin/Bass productions cartoons from the 80's; Kenneth specializes in narrative-centered cartooning and illustrations.

Color & Rendering: Joaquin Pereyra

Bio: Joaquin graduated from Provincial University of Córdoba in Cordoba, Argentina with a degree in graphic design. He's been working in the comic book industry since 2010, where he began as an assistant colorist with Michael Kelleher (Kellustration) in comic reconstruction for Marvel Comics and Dark Horse (Marvel Masterworks & archives). After a few years of gaining experience, Joaquin developed different artistic styles and was involved in several higher caliber projects, such as Assassins Creed (alternate covers), Alex Rider "Ark Angel," Bandai/Namco "Man of Medan" 2020 (in-game comic book), and he also created some promotional art for Sony, Disney, and Marvel.

Publisher: Dr. Sonia Cunningham Leverette

Bio: Amazon.com and AfricanBookstore.net Bestselling Children's Book Author Sonia has penned over 10 books and has published nearly 100. She is passionate about Christ, people and books. After a 30-year career in education as an English teacher and school and district-level administrator, Sonia enjoys assisting authors in seeing their dreams come to life. A current resident of Greenville County, SC, she is a native of Laurens, SC. Visit HadassahsCrownPublishing.com to see her and other authors' works and to receive updates about new publications.

HadassahsCrownPublishing.com
Publishing Excellence with Integrity

www.ingramcontent.com/pod-product-compliance
Lightning Source LLC
Chambersburg PA
CBHW042110090526

44592CB00004B/69